Harewood

*"I would not exceed the limits of expense that I have always set myself.
Let us do everything properly and well, mais pas trop".*

EDWIN LASCELLES TO ROBERT ADAM

Introduction

THIS 'NEW' GUIDEBOOK to Harewood House is, like much of the House itself, something of a hybrid. Much of it was written by my late father, the 7th Earl of Harewood, for the previous guidebook. He moved into the House with his parents in 1929 and lived here until his death in 2011, more than 80 years. He inherited the title in 1947, which means he was Lord Harewood for 64 years, far longer than any other incumbent. So I think it's pretty safe to say that no-one has ever known the House better than him and therefore wholly appropriate that his words should lead you through its rooms. You could have no better guide.

I have written the new History of Harewood that begins this book. We have learnt much that is new in recent years, especially about the period before Harewood House was built in the mid 18th century. I've also made some interventions in the text for the rooms, where their uses have changed or where the descriptions are no longer accurate. There are also essays by other voices, notably my father's great friend Richard Buckle who wrote the 1980 version of the guidebook

Harewood is and always has been a living, changing place, reflecting the views, tastes and lifestyles of its inhabitants. 18th century English gentleman's country house. Victorian family home. Royal household. Wartime convalescent hospital. Major tourist destination. Harewood has been all those things and more. It is now run as an educational charitable trust, for the public benefit, making the House and its collections accessible and, we hope, interesting to as wide a range of people as possible.

There is always something new to discover here, whether you've lived at Harewood all your life or are visiting for the first time. Enjoy your visit. Come again. Tell your friends. We need you to help us keep it alive.

David Lascelles, *Earl of Harewood*

Harewood – a History

BY DAVID LASCELLES

Until recently, much of the telling of Harewood's history has focused on Harewood House, its builders and inhabitants. But the House is a relatively new arrival here, an 18th century interloper on a very ancient landscape. In the last few years we've learnt many new things about the history of Harewood before the building of the House, raising questions as well as finding answers. So this history is, as in the end all histories are, a combination of fact and speculation, my own interpretation of the long story of Harewood, from ancient times to the present day.

Ancient Harewood

The earliest sign of human activity at Harewood is on a large boulder of millstone grit, The Greystone, high on the far hillside as you look across the Lake from Harewood House. Pecked onto its surface with a stone tool or possibly a deer antler is a large cup and ring mark dating back to the Neolithic and Bronze Age, more than 4000 years ago. There are conflicting theories about the meaning of these marks: they might signify the site of a burial ground or a place where rituals were performed; or they might, as the spectacular view across the surrounding countryside suggests, be signposts or landmarks for travellers across the ancient landscape of northern England.

The first known owners of Harewood are three Saxon Chieftains, the wonderfully named Tor, Sprot and Grim. Their names are recorded in the Domesday Book, William the Conqueror's massive and extraordinarily comprehensive survey of land ownership compiled shortly after the Battle of Hastings. It told him who owned what, down to the last pig and cow, what the land and buildings were worth and what tax was therefore payable. It was the key to his aim of dominating and controlling medieval England. Tor, Sprot and Grim, their loyalty to the Norman invaders in serious doubt, were among the casualties. Their land was confiscated and given to a Norman nobleman, Robert de Romelli, whose descendants were therefore the first Lords of the Manor of Harewood.

Harewood Castle

The oldest building at Harewood is Harewood Castle. A major programme of repair and consolidation of the surviving structure took place during 2004 and 2005, with financial support from English Heritage, Yorkshire Television, and the Harewood Estate. A considerable body of new information, both architectural and archaeological, was gathered, which has prompted a number of new interpretations, as well as challenging some of the existing theories.

In 1366 a 'license to crenellate' (to fortify) was granted to Sir William de Aldeburgh, who had inherited the manor of Harewood by marriage a few years earlier. Substantial earthworks around the ruins of the castle (still only partially explored) indicate there were earlier buildings on the site, but de Aldeburgh made a decision to demolish and replace whatever was there with something brand new – foreshadowing Gawthorpe Hall and Harewood House some 400 years later.

Harewood Castle was designed to strike a balance between security and comfort: a *"mixture of convenience and magnificence"*, more accurately described as a fortified Tower House than a castle. Some of its features – the portcullis over the main entrance, the narrow arrow slit windows, the remains of metal grilles over the larger windows - indicate a concern for defence. Others were primarily about comfort, aesthetics or status. The mullioned and transomed window frames, for example, are fine examples of 14th century masons' skills and though the massively thick walls would have made the castle eminently defensible, they also contained an elaborate network of internal walkways, stairs and flues. Even the dramatic setting on a steep north-facing slope with spectacular views up and down Wharfedale, was as much about status as security: early sighting of any approaching

Harewood Castle
from the Southeast
JMW Turner
1798, watercolour. ◠

Gawthorpe

The neighbouring estate to Harewood was Gawthorpe and its 13th century manor house, Gawthorpe Hall, was home for thirteen generations to the Gascoigne family. The most eminent of them was Sir William Gascoigne, who became Chief Justice of England in 1401 and is immortalised by Shakespeare in *Henry IV Part 2* as the judge who sends Prince Hal, the future Henry V, to prison for unruly behaviour.

The two estates co-existed quite happily for some time it seemed, with Gascoignes marrying both Redmaynes and Rythers. The exact date of the Gascoignes becoming the dominant partner is uncertain, but as a 19th century historian puts it: *"The Gascoignes appear to have been a prudent and thriving family; the Rythers the reverse; and by the natural effects of such conduct, the vassal supplanted the lord."* As good a theory as any I suppose.

In 1580 the now combined estate passed by marriage to the politically influential Wentworth family, but their fortunes went into serious decline when, in 1641, Thomas Wentworth, Earl of Strafford was executed by Charles I for treason. Heavily in debt, Strafford's son sold Harewood Castle, Gawthorpe Hall and the attached estates to Sir John Cutler, a self-made London merchant. The satirist Alexander Pope mocked Cutler, perhaps unfairly, as a miser and a skinflint:

"A few grey hairs his reverend temple crowned, t'was very want that sold them for two pound."

It was Cutler's relative and the executor of his will, John Boulter, who sold the Gawthorpe and Harewood estates to the Lascelles family in 1738.

Gawthorpe Hall was pulled down and turfed over soon after Harewood House was completed in 1771 and the building effectively disappeared, known only from two early 18th century prints. Then, in 2009, with the help of the University of York Archaeology Department, we started excavations on the South Front, the large field running down from Harewood House to the Lake, revealing Gawthorpe's exact location, previously thought to be under

trouble certainly, but also dominating the immediate landscape in a way designed to impress. Surrounding it or attached to it would have been other buildings such as barns and stables, as well as landscaped gardens, designed for leisure as much as practicality.

When de Aldeburgh's son died in 1391, he left no male heir and the estate passed to his two daughters, Sybil and Elizabeth. They and their husbands Sir William Ryther and Sir Richard Redmayne shared occupation of the Castle, either simultaneously or in a 14th century version of time-share, an arrangement the two families continued for more than 200 years.

The last resident was Robert Ryther, who retired to his wife's family's estate in Lincolnshire around 1630. By 1657, when the amalgamated Harewood and Gawthorpe estates were bought by Sir John Cutler, the Castle was falling down and uninhabitable. Did the Rythers simply lock the door and walk away, leaving the building to its fate, its stone and timbers to be cannibalised for use elsewhere on the estate, its gardens to become neglected and overgrown, its ornamental ponds to silt up and drain away? Perhaps it had simply become too old fashioned, unmanageable and uncomfortable to live in any more. Nobody knows.

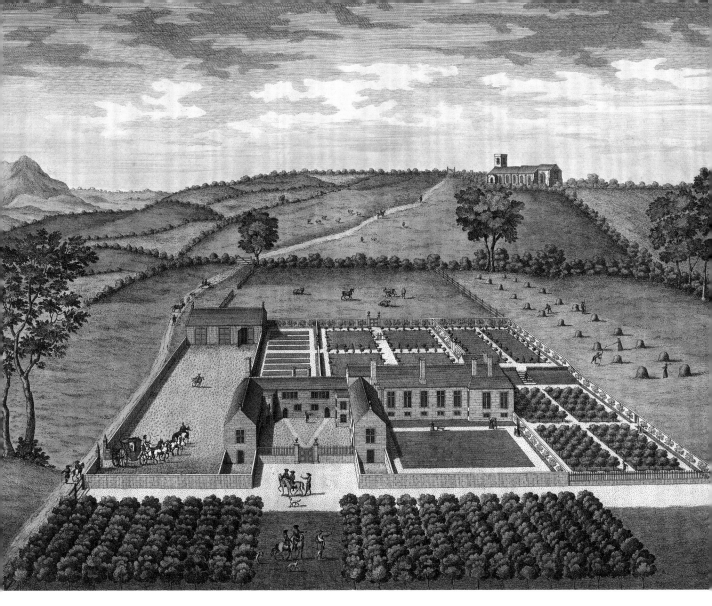

Gawthorpe Hall from the South
Engraving c. 1720. ↺

Harewood House, 'the new house at Gawthorpe', would be near the big tree in front of All Saints Church (top right). Almscliff Crag (top left) seems to have turned into Mount Vesuvius.

Gawthorpe Hall from the North
Engraving c. 1720. ↻

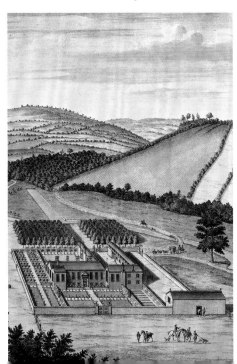

the Lake. Its foundations are now clearly visible for the first time since its demolition. It was a substantial building, a handsome medieval manor house with a frontage of more than 60 metres, a double-height great hall and chapel, and elaborate formal gardens, all of which had been added to and adapted over its more than 400 years of occupancy. Edwin Lascelles, builder of Harewood House, lived there for more than 30 years while his new home was being built and attempted some modernisations himself. For a short while Gawthorpe and Harewood House co-existed, before Edwin had Gawthorpe knocked down. No conservation officers to stop that happening in the 1770s. Besides, it was spoiling the view.

Gawthorpe's demolition was total and abrupt. As a consequence, the dig has already uncovered many fascinating artefacts: pottery, glass, seals with the Lascelles family crest, stone gargoyles, a flint arrow head and a delicate silver ring, among others. The project is ongoing, but we are learning more all the time, revealing a little new history each year.

7

All Saints Church

The building that spans all of Harewood's known history, from Norman times to the present day, is All Saints Church. We have a precise date for its foundation. When the roof was replaced in the 18th century this inscription was found cut into a beam: *"We adore and praise thee thou holy Jesus, because thou hast redeemed us by thy Holy Cross, 1116".* The founder was William de Curcy, son-in-law of Robert de Romelli, the Norman Baron to whom the manor of Harewood was given by William the Conqueror after the Battle of Hastings.

This original church was completely rebuilt in the 15th century by the descendants of Sir William de Aldeburgh (the builder of Harewood Castle), and altered again in the late 18th century, both by John Carr, the architect of Harewood House, and by Edwin Lascelles' surveyor John Belwood. These changes were not universally admired: *"About the year 1793, a series of most barbarous alterations were carried into effect, which, to say the least of them, reflect discredit upon those who were concerned in them",* thunders John Jones in his 'History of Harewood' of 1859. Stained-glass windows were removed and sold, carved oak seats replaced by pews, the oak open roof replaced by deal rafters. Shortly after John Jones' rant, the Victorian architect Sir Gilbert Scott altered some of the alterations so what you see today is something of a hybrid.

But the outstanding feature of Harewood Church is its magnificent collection of alabaster tombs, often said to be the finest in England outside a cathedral. They are the most vivid evidence we have of Harewood's ancient history, showing six lords and ladies from the families who owned the Harewood and Gawthorpe estates during the 15th and early 16th century: Redmaynes, Rythers and Gascoignes. The oldest is of Chief Justice Gascoigne, who died in 1419, and the last is of Edward Redmayne, who died in 1510, and his wife Elizabeth.

The pale, glowing alabaster figures would have looked very different then. They would have been brightly coloured (you can still see traces of paint in the carved folds of their garments) and some would have been covered by canopies (removed in the 18th century). They were restored in the 1970s with support from the Redundant Churches Fund and moved to their present positions. Looked at carefully they are full of character, portraits of real people, not just formal depictions of lords and ladies of rank and status.

All Saints has not been active since the late 1960s, but the Lascelles family vault is there. The Church is still used occasionally for concerts, baptisms or memorial services, most recently in honour of my father after his death in the summer of 2011, a memorable musical occasion.

Alabaster tombs in Harewood Church. ◠

The Village

Harewood Village is mentioned in the Domesday Book as the largest of eight settlements in the parish. By the early 13th century it was the centre of local legal, administrative, agricultural and ecclesiastical activity, *"a great thoroughfare town"* with a market every Monday and a Fair every July. Very little of this ancient village remains, just a couple of cottages and some street names. It was completely rebuilt by John Carr, the architect of Harewood House, and his assistant Peter Atkinson between 1750 and 1820. Carr and his patron, Edwin Lascelles, created a model village, unusual in being socially inclusive with house sizes and rents to suit every pocket – from £49 a year at the top end down to a few shillings for the less well off – and praised by contemporaries for its *"comfortable habitations that reflect great honour and praise on their noble owner"*. It was strategically placed, with two turnpike roads running through it, from Wharfedale in the north towards Leeds and east-west from Tadcaster towards Otley. In 1753 an attempt to

charge a toll to cross Harewood Bridge led to a violent confrontation between protestors and Edwin's tenants and farm workers, which a few days later escalated into a full-scale riot in Briggate in Leeds, with the army called out and eight left dead and fifty wounded.

By the late 18th century the village had six pubs and by 1850 there was a Savings Bank and a Literary & Scientific Institute, which had a sizeable library and offered evening classes and regular lectures. A village cricket club was founded, with a ground that is still played on, to the south of the drive to Harewood House.

Now two busy commuter roads, close to the routes of the old turnpikes, bisect the village and there are 20th century mews developments tucked away behind Carr's elegant rows of cottages. To approach Harewood House today, you still must drive through the Doric arch of the main gates, known as The Lodge, at the end of Harewood Avenue, designed in the late 18th century by Humphrey Repton (though he was far from happy when Carr adapted and re-positioned it without consultation).

Harewood Village
John Varley
c. 1800, watercolour. ↻

Edward Lascelles
Unknown artist, *c. 1730.*

The successful trader, dressed in his finest, with a ship carrying sugar from the West Indies to Europe in full sail behind him. ⌕

How the Lascelles came to Harewood

There was a village called Lassele in Normandy and a Picotus de Lacelle fought in the Norman army at the Battle of Hastings. Unfortunately for historical neatness, he wasn't the Norman noble who was gifted the estates of Harewood previously owned by Tor, Sprot and Grim, but King William rewarded de Lacelle with land in North Yorkshire, not so far away. It was here that the family established themselves over the following centuries as reasonably successful if not especially distinguished gentleman farmers. The most controversial figure was Francis Lascelles; a colonel in Cromwell's Parliamentary Army and a seemingly reluctant member of the Commission who tried Charles I. Francis absented himself from the crucial sessions and did not sign the King's death warrant.

It is with Francis' grandson Henry that the story of Harewood and the Lascelles family really begins. The Lascelles already had interests in the West Indies when Henry first went to Barbados in 1711. He was just 21. It was a time when great fortunes were being made on the backs of the enslaved Africans shipped over to the Caribbean and the Americas in the most appalling conditions before being put to work on the plantations that produced luxury goods for the European market: sugar, cotton, rum, tobacco. The wealth of many of Britain's great institutions – the Church, the Royal Family, banks, artistic and educational establishments – was either created or greatly enhanced during that period.

Henry set out to control every aspect of the sugar trade, what we now would call vertical integration; very astute, however much we now abhor the business he was in. He was part owner of several slave ships (full ownership was too risky; many ships along with their human cargo sank or were intercepted by pirates). He was banker to plantation owners, becoming a plantation owner – and so a slave owner himself – as his clients defaulted on their loan payments. With his partners, he owned distribution warehouses in London. He acquired exclusive rights to supply the Royal Navy when they docked in Barbados. He was Collector of Customs for the Barbadian port of Bridgetown, one of the most valuable revenue posts in the entire British Customs Service. The Customs job was clearly one that could lead to 'conflicts of interest'. Business morals were very different then, but even so Henry and his business partner and brother Edward were tried on corruption charges in the 1730s. They were cleared, but some of the mud stuck. Like many hugely successful people, he was not well liked by his contemporaries.

But for Henry it must have all seemed worthwhile. Within a matter of 20 years or so he had become one of the richest men in England. He made sure that his eldest son Edwin, born in Barbados in 1712, received the kind of classical education he never had: Cambridge University and the European grand tour. Together they started to buy parcels of land, and in 1738 they acquired the estates of Harewood and Gawthorpe, where Edwin was later to build Harewood House.

Henry didn't live to see it. He killed himself in 1753, six years before building began, by – I quote from a contemporary's letter – cutting his *"throat and arms and across his belly"*.

Harewood House is full of portraits, including one of Henry's brother Edward who was very much the junior partner in their business enterprises. But there is no image of Henry Lascelles, the man without whom none of it would have been possible.

1807-2007

2007 was the Bicentenary of the Abolition of the Slave Trade in the British Empire. It was clear to me that this was not something we at Harewood could simply let pass by, to contribute by omission to what has been called 'a collective national amnesia' about this terrible episode in British history. We had decided some years previously that we had to try to discover more about the exact nature of the Lascelles family's involvement with the sugar trade and the slave trade. Much of the story of Henry Lascelles – touched on here in a very abbreviated form – is based on research done by the University of York History Department. A book was published, *Slavery, Family and Gentry Capitalism in the British Atlantic – the World of the Lascelles, 1648-1834,* funded with grants from Harewood House Trust and the Leverhulme Trust. Though many of the papers dealing with the business affairs of Henry and his partners were destroyed in a German bombing raid on London in 1940, we discovered more, mostly untouched since the 18th century, during an inventory at Harewood House in the 1990s. During 2007, with the help of a grant from the Heritage Lottery Fund, a start was made in conserving and digitising these papers, many of them in an extremely fragile condition, at the Borthwick Institute at the University of York. The results are now available online.

We were also aware that we needed to deal with the legacy of the slave trade in Britain today. Our Education and Audience Development Department worked with schools and community groups to deliver a wide range of talks, tours and lectures. We ran a programme of contemporary art centred on various artists' responses to the legacy of the slave trade, including an exhibition of masks and sculptures from West Africa and a specially commissioned film shot in Harewood and Barbados by the artist Sonia Boyce. Abolition Day itself was marked by a service held by the Chapeltown Baptist Church in Harewood Church. We mounted a series of performances of *Carnival*

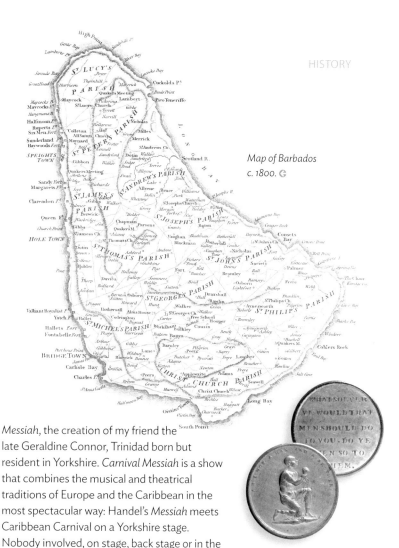

Map of Barbados c. 1800.

Messiah, the creation of my friend the late Geraldine Connor, Trinidad born but resident in Yorkshire. *Carnival Messiah* is a show that combines the musical and theatrical traditions of Europe and the Caribbean in the most spectacular way: Handel's *Messiah* meets Caribbean Carnival on a Yorkshire stage. Nobody involved, on stage, back stage or in the audience, will ever forget the experience.

The source of the wealth that built Harewood is historical fact. There is nothing anyone can do to change the past, however appalling or regrettable that past might be. What we can do, however, what we must do, is engage with that legacy and in so doing stand a chance of having a positive effect on the future.

Abolition medallions c. 1806.

Carnival Messiah at Harewood, 2007.

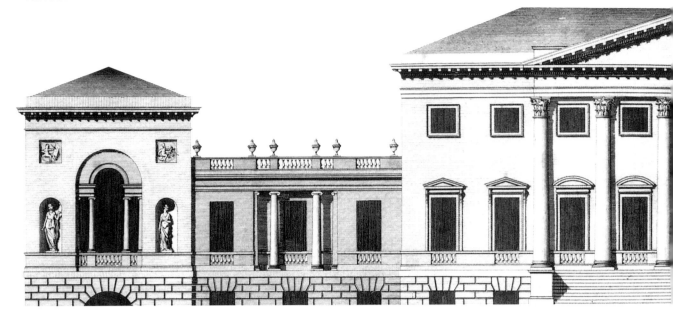

Building Harewood

In an earlier version of the guidebook, my father wrote:

"**Edwin Lascelles** was quite clearly a difficult customer with what is euphemistically known as a mind of his own. He was over forty when his father died and immediately set about realising the plans, which must have been maturing in his mind for years. After rejecting plans submitted by William Chambers, he commissioned **John Carr** of York to design the house. Carr's work at Harewood was extensive, starting with the Stables and continuing with the House, farm, model village and numerous other buildings on the estate. In 1758, while Carr was working on the Stable block, Edwin showed the plans to **Robert Adam**, the young Scottish architect who was in the process of establishing himself in London after three years of extensive study in Italy. Adam found little to alter in Carr's plans. Nonetheless, he wrote to his brother James *'I have thrown in large, semi-circular back courts with columns betwixt the house and the wings.'* James replied *'It affords me the greatest pleasure that you have tickled it up to dazzle the eyes of the squire.'* Not much remains of Adam's architectural alterations: Edwin rejected one of the courts and the design for the other one proved to be structurally unsound and so was never built.

Edwin's steward was Samuel Popplewell, responsible for the general management of the estate, but he seems to have had a hard time with his master, who wrote *'I presume to be as good a judge of the management of my affairs as you, and if I am conscious of a great expense, and what done for it doth not appear adequate, who hath a better right to find fault than myself. I think they have been too hasty in beginning to build.'* And to Adam, more temperately, but no less firmly: *'I would not exceed the limits of expense that I have always set myself. Let us do everything properly and well, mais pas trop'.*

If Adam's effect on the exterior of the House was limited, he seems to have had something like a free hand in the State Room interiors and, in spite of some later alterations; it remains one of his great achievements. His hand can be seen everywhere: in ceilings and carpets; in elaborate decoration on almost any flat surface; in the choice of Joseph Rose and William Collins for the plasterwork, of Angelica Kauffman, Antonio Zucchi and Biagio Rebecca to paint the decorative panels on ceilings and walls, and most important of all, of Thomas Chippendale to supply the furniture. Adam's is the controlling mind, but I suppose it would only be fair in assessing the results to bracket his flair and taste with the sense of proportion, imagination and indomitable will of Edwin who set it all in motion.

Edwin Lascelles (*detail*)
Joshua Reynolds, 1768. ⟳

North elevation of
Harewood House
John Carr, 1771. ⟳⟳

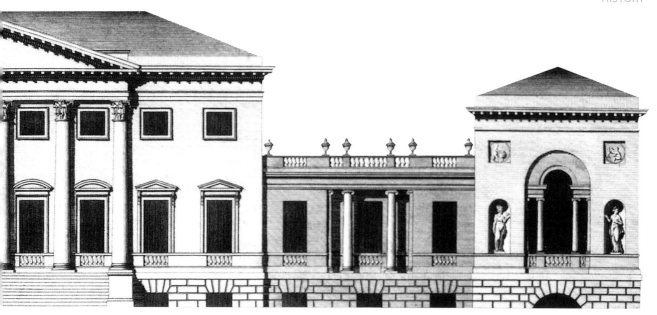

The foundation stone was laid in January 1759, Adam's decorative schemes date from 1765, the House became habitable in 1771 and the Gallery, its grandest room, was finished in 1772."

GEORGE HAREWOOD (GH) 1994

Robert Adam
George Willison, 1774.
Courtesy of the National Portrait Gallery.

Designs for the interior of Harewood House
Robert Adam, c. 1765.

John Carr
William Beechey, 1791.
Courtesy of the National Portrait Gallery.

Capability Brown
Nathaniel Dance , *1769.*
Courtesy of the National Portrait Gallery.

In the same year **Capability Brown**, the most renowned designer of English landscape (himself an architect), submitted plans for the Park, surrounding the Lake with plantations and gently undulating parkland where before had been fields and pasture. For nine years Brown worked on the Park and was paid over £6,000, a big sum for those days. What he liked to do was to point up the possibilities of nature, by regulating the natural curves of the ground (hundreds of men were employed to shift earth from one place to another) and by judicious planting. At the turn of the century another great landscape designer, Humphrey Repton, added some ideas, but time, which fells even the mightiest of trees, and wind, which can destroy whole acres of planting (we lost nearly 30,000 trees in two days of gale in 1962), inevitably affect plans like Brown's and Repton's. Nonetheless, most of what they shaped and planted and a good deal of what they aimed for is still in working order at Harewood. *GH, 1994*

Thomas Chippendale (1718-1789) born a few miles away in Otley, worked at Harewood from 1767 and was responsible for the furniture and furnishings throughout the House. This was his largest and most lucrative commission, fulfilled from his workshop in St Martin's Lane in London and worth more than £10,000 by the time of its completion in 1797. He was a frequent collaborator with Robert Adam and, under his influence, he brought the design of English furniture to new levels of sophistication. Perhaps for the first time, what was made in this country rivalled the more elaborate products of France, and his best furniture possesses a simplicity of line which is hard to find in its French equivalents. The commission to furnish Harewood left no room untouched: sofas, mirrors, beds, chairs, tables, lanterns, clothes presses, cupboards, soft furnishings and pelmets; from the most exquisite 'parade' furniture designed as part of Adam's coordinated interior schemes, to garden benches and simple but elegant chairs for the Steward's Room below stairs.

Chippendale died 18 years before the final commissions were completed, and the firm passed to his son, Thomas Chippendale the Younger, whose work can be seen in the Cinnamon Drawing Room and Gallery.

During major alterations in the 1840s, a number of pieces of Chippendale furniture were dismantled and put into storage where they remained untouched until the mid 1980s. These included the State Bed and several mirrors, which were stripped of their elaborate peripheral ornamentation, leaving only the oval frames on the wall. Christopher Gilbert, in his *Life and Work of Thomas Chippendale* (1978), illustrates some of these pieces as they were before an extensive programme of sorting and repair was undertaken in the early 1990s. This was a very complex project, piecing together literally hundreds of ornamental fragments from each mirror, a considerable feat of detective work as well as craftsmanship by the furniture restoration specialists Carvers and Gilders.
The results can be seen in the State Bedroom, the Yellow Drawing Room and the Cinnamon Drawing Room. *DL, 2012*

Detail of Diana and Minerva commode (State Bedroom).

Detail of commode in the Chinese style (East Bedroom).

Working drawing of a tea table, 1773.

Detail of mirror ornamentation (Yellow Drawing Room).

Harewood House
Thomas Malton, 1778.

The Changing House

Edwin, Carr, Adam, Chippendale and Brown were the creators of Harewood House and its grounds, and their vision is still largely what you see here. But theirs are far from being the only marks left over the past 250 years.

Succession at Harewood got off to an uneasy start. Edwin married twice, but had no male heir, so when he died in 1795 he was succeeded by his cousin Edward, who became the 1st Earl of Harewood when the title was created by an Act of Parliament in 1812. Edward's oldest son, also called Edward, became the first of Harewood's great collectors of works of art. Edward Viscount Lascelles, nicknamed 'Beau', was clearly a young man of taste and style, part of the Prince of Wales' fashionable set; they were mistaken for each other on more than one occasion. He was not just a follower of fashion however. He had both a good eye and the financial resources to capitalise on it. He is responsible for Harewood's fine collection of Sèvres porcelain, much of which he bought at the auction houses of revolutionary Paris which

were selling off the collections of French aristocrats who had gone to the guillotine. No class solidarity there.

Beau also had the vision to commission two young artists to make watercolours – then still considered an ephemeral and avant-garde medium – of Harewood House and its landscape. The first was Thomas Girtin, who died shortly after but is considered one of England's finest watercolourists. The other was JMW Turner, one of the greatest artists England has ever produced. In 1797, aged only 22, Turner was almost unknown, with a small

reputation as an architectural draftsman. He later acknowledged this trip to Yorkshire as a formative moment in his career.

Beau Lascelles died before his father, so the title passed to his younger brother Henry. Henry was not a collector, but lived through some interesting political times. For some years he was one of Yorkshire's two Members of Parliament and his colleague was William Wilberforce, best known of course as the driving force behind the movement to abolish the slave trade. Wilberforce visited Harewood on several occasions.

Harewood House from the Southwest
JMW Turner, *1798*.

Edward 'Beau' Lascelles
John Hoppner, *1797*.

Henry, 2nd Earl of Harewood
Thomas Lawrence, *1823*.

Barry's elevation of Harewood House, 1848. ↻

Louisa, 3rd Countess of Harewood
George Richmond, c. 1855. ↻

Louisa, very much the formidable Victorian matriarch, stands with a proprietorial air on the Terrace Barry has built for her.

The Terrace
Roger Fenton, Photograph, 1860. ↻

Fenton was a pioneer of location (as opposed to studio) photography, best known for his pictures of the Crimean War, so sometimes called the first war photographer.

There is a vivid description by Humphrey Repton, the landscape designer, of a weekend party in 1799. Repton comments on Wilberforce's fine singing voice and describes a boat trip on the Lake where Wilberforce and Henry each take an oar. They end up at Harewood's newly constructed greenhouses and Repton describes Wilberforce's expression as they look at a sugar cane sapling together: *"We could read in his glistening eye all the complicated train of thought which had called forth his extraordinary energy and engaged his deep attention for so many years."*

By far the most visible intervention at Harewood was by the Victorians. The 3rd Earl married Louisa Thynne, daughter of the Marquis of Bath, owner of the Longleat estate in southwest England. They had 13 children and Louisa clearly thought Harewood was neither big nor grand enough for such a large family. What was required was no longer an English gentleman's country house, but a Victorian family home. Louisa called in Charles Barry – best known as the architect of the Houses of Parliament in London - to oversee the changes. Work began in 1845. Several of the rooms were substantially altered, and some of Adam's original decorative schemes done away with altogether. An extra storey was built, adding more bedrooms and servant quarters. The classical portico to the south was removed. Most dramatically, a large Italianate Terrace – very much the fashion of the time – was added, to make a transition between the House and the carefully constructed 'naturalness' of Capability Brown's landscape.

According to my father *"the most positive thing the 4th Earl did for Harewood was to marry Elizabeth de Burgh the grand-daughter of the Prime Minister George Canning."* Some 70 years after their wedding, this family connection bore surprising and significant fruit.

Elizabeth's younger brother Hubert, 2nd Marquess of Clanricarde, was not a well-liked man. He was the kind of brutal absentee landlord that made the Irish rural poor hate the English, was notoriously mean despite his considerable personal wealth, and seemed to be on bad terms with all his family, especially his nephew the 5th Earl of Harewood. The story goes that Hubert was in his London club, eating alone as usual, when he was approached by his great-nephew Harry, my grandfather, later to become the 6th Earl. Harry was on convalescent leave from the 1st World War and asked the old miser if he would join him for dinner. Hubert was so pleased to be treated with some degree of warmth by a member of his family, that, when he died soon afterwards, he missed a generation and left Harry everything in his will. (There's a moral there, as you may well have spotted.)

Harry used the money imaginatively, investing in paintings, especially works by some of the great masters of the Renaissance: Titian, Bellini, El Greco, Veronese and Tintoretto among others. There are other great collections of Renaissance art in English country houses, but Harewood's is the only one acquired in the 20th century. In 1922 Harry married Princess Mary, daughter of King George V, and in 1923 my father was born, christened George (for his maternal grandfather) Henry (because Lascelles boys always were) Hubert (after Harry's great-uncle and benefactor). His parents oversaw many changes in the House. Between 1929, when Harry became the 6th Earl and he and Princess Mary moved to Harewood, and 1939, when the 2nd World War intervened and the House became a convalescent hospital (as it had been during the 1st World War), they instigated a series of restoration projects. Rooms were refurbished and pictures re-hung; Chippendale's furniture was re-upholstered and sets reunited, so that Robert Adam's carefully coordinated decorative schemes re-emerged and the House started to look once again like the one its creators had planned.

The Wedding of Henry, Viscount Lascelles and Princess Mary, *with the bride's parents, King George V and Queen Mary, on either side of them, 1922.* ⊙

Henry, 'Harry', and Princess Mary *with their much loved dogs on the Terrace, taken in 1946, shortly before Harry's death.* ⊙

George, 7th Earl of Harewood and Patricia, Countess of Harewood
Cecil Beaton, *photograph, 1971.* ⊙

During the 1930s, with a Princess in residence, Harewood was a Royal household as well as a family home, but the end of the 2nd World War and the death of the 6th Earl a couple of years later changed everything. My father became Lord Harewood at the age of only 24 with crippling death duties to pay. He remembers the family solicitor laying out a map of the estate with Harewood House in the middle, taking out a compass and pencil and drawing a circle. *"Everything outside this will have to be sold"*, he was told. Furniture and pictures went under the auctioneer's hammer as well as land and the gardens were made less labour intensive by, among other measures, grassing over Charles Barry's Italianate parterre (restored in 1991).

A period of consolidation followed, but my father never allowed things to stagnate. The House and grounds were opened to the public. The first guidebook of the modern era was

published in 1959. By the late 1960s plans were afoot for a Bird Garden and Adventure Playground (both opened in 1970) to make Harewood more attractive to families with children. In 1976, Jacob Epstein's magnificent sculpture *Adam* took up residence in the Hall, a piece of 20th century art standing alongside the historic collection. In 1986, the House and Gardens were made into an Educational Charitable Trust, run for the public benefit. My father and his second wife Patricia began a major programme of restoration, completing the work, as my father saw it, that his parents had begun 50 years earlier. In 1989, my wife Diane instigated the transformation of the Sub-Hall into the Terrace Gallery; the first designated contemporary art space in an English country house. In 2004 we opened Below Stairs, the kitchens and servants' quarters, once the engine room of the House. The last major room restoration – the re-hanging of 18th century Chinese wallpaper in the East Bedroom – took place in 2008.

And so it goes on. Harewood's history is still evolving – always changing, always striving to stay relevant to the present day – as, actually, it always has. Today, Harewood House can no longer be somewhere that exists solely for the benefit of a single, privileged family. Nor can it be somewhere that is frozen in time. It must be alive, cared for by the people who inhabit it and enjoyed by the people who visit it. Harewood's is a living history, one with many stories still to tell. *DL, 2012*

Harewood Estate tenants and staff *1950. Princess Mary in the centre with the wide-brimmed hat, my father and mother on either side of her.*

Timeline of Events

1753
Edwin Lascelles
inherits Harewood

1797
JMW Turner first
visits and paints
Harewood House

HENRY LASCELLES
3rd Earl of Harewood
(1797–1857)

Lady Louisa Thynne
Countess of
Harewood

1759
Foundation stone
of Harewood House
laid

c. **1805**
Beau Lascelles
collecting Sèvres
porcelain

1767
**Thomas
Chippendale**
begins the 30-year
commission, the
largest of his life, to
furnish Harewood
House

1812
Building work on
Harewood village
completed

HENRY LASCEL...
4th Earl of Harew...
(1824–1892)
m. 1 **Lady Elizab...
de Burgh**
m. 2 **Diana Smy...**

1738
Henry Lascelles
acquires the Manor
of Gawthorpe and
Harewood

1771 Harewood
House completed

1774
Gawthorpe
Hall
demolished

EDWARD LASCELLES
1st Earl of Harewood
(1740–1820)

Anne Chaloner
Countess of
Harewood

1845
Henry, 4th Viscount
Lascelles marries
Elizabeth de Burgh
(great niece of
George Canning
who was Prime
Minister 1827)

1844-1848
Charles Barry
begins work on
modernising
Harewood House
under the direction
of Louisa, 3rd
Countess of
Harewood

EDWIN LASCELLES
Lord Harewood
(1712–1795)

HENRY LASCELLES
2nd Earl of Harewood
(1767–1841)

Henrietta Sebright
Countess of
Harewood

1721
Sir Robert Walpole
becomes first British
Prime Minister

1746
Jacobites are
defeated at
Culloden, the last
battle on British soil

1775-1783
The American
Revolutionary War,
leading to the
Declaration of
Independence in 1776

1807
Abolition of the
transatlantic slave
trade

1833
Emancipation of the
West Indian slave
trade

1700
Start of the European
Enlightenment that
sought to mobilise the
power of reason, in
order to reform society
and advance
knowledge

1746-1755
Samuel Johnson
compiles his
*Dictionary of the
English Language*

1760
Start of the
Industrial
Revolution

1789
Storming of
the Bastille.
Start of the French
Revolution

1815
Battle of Waterloo.
Napoleon exiled
on St Helena

1857
First war of In...
Independ...

1859
Charles Dar...
publishes *Or...
Origin of Spe...*

| 1700 | 1725 | 1750 | 1775 | 1800 | 1825 | 1850 |

HENRY LASCELLES
5th Earl of Harewood
(1846–1929)

Lady Florence Bridgeman
Countess of Harewood

GEORGE LASCELLES
7th Earl of Harewood
(1923–2011)
m. 1 **Marion Stein**

Patricia Tuckwell
Countess of Harewood

1984
The Harewood House Trust, an educational charitable trust, is established

2004
Building of the Harewood Stupa and creation of the Himalayan Garden

2007
Carnival Messiah at Harewood

Lady Elizabeth de Burgh

1916
Henry, 6th Viscount Lascelles inherits fortune from his great uncle, 2nd Marquess of Clanricarde

1939
Harewood becomes a convalescent hospital for soldiers during World War II

1965
HRH Princess Mary dies at Harewood

1989
The Terrace Gallery opens, the first designated contemporary art space in an English country house

1922
Henry, 6th Viscount Lascelles marries HRH Princess Mary at Westminster Abbey

1950
Harewood House and grounds opens to the public

1976
Jacob Epstein's *Adam* arrives at Harewood

HENRY LASCELLES
6th Earl of Harewood
(1882–1947)

HRH Princess Mary, The Princess Royal Countess of Harewood

DAVID LASCELLES
8th Earl of Harewood
(1950–   )
m. 1 **Margaret Messenger**

Diane Howse
Countess of Harewood

1879
Thomas Edison invents practical electric light

1917
The Russian Revolution

1939-1945
Second World War

1963
The start of the Civil Rights Movement in the USA

1989
The fall of the Berlin Wall

2001
Attacks on the World Trade Center and the Pentagon

1918
British women over 30 win the right to vote

1949
Communist party leaders proclaim The People's Republic of China

1973
Great Britain joins the European Economic Community

1994
End of apartheid system in South Africa. Nelson Mandela elected president

1895
Louis Lumière and his brother present the first public cinema screening

1914-1918
First World War

1947
India and Pakistan become independent nations

1875 *1900* *1925* *1950* *1975* *2000* *2025*

The House

The Hall

A column painted to imitate porphyry, with a Chippendale hall chair in front. ⟳

THE HALLS of houses Adam designed tend towards the heroic and Harewood is no exception; witness the columns which seem to refer back to an earlier architectural age. At Harewood, Adam designed the ceilings, friezes and chimneypieces throughout the House, and his habit was to aim at an overall decorative scheme with everything part of a unified design. (In the Hall for instance the ox skulls, a feature of the frieze, recur over the doors and on the chimneypiece carved in marble). He outlined his schemes in some detail but left their realisation to the stuccoists, Joseph Rose and William Collins, whose own fantasy was engaged to some purpose – the wedding of Neptune and Amphitrite is the subject of the oblong relief over the fireplace with the Chariot of Phaeton opposite, where was once a second fireplace.

As Adam conceived it, the Hall was a noble ante-chamber rather than a place in which to linger, but the inventory made in 1795 suggests

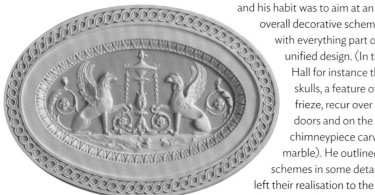

Detail of plasterwork by Joseph Rose. ⟳

that 25 years after the House was first occupied it was already used as somewhere to sit, not just pass through. Certainly that was how the Victorians employed it and by the end of the century photographs show it heavily furnished, the plaster statues replaced in the niches by busts on pedestals, with palms in pots on either side of the internal door and antlers flanking the fireplace.

We have tried a measure of restoration. The columns were painted to imitate porphyry, as described in John Jewell's guide book of 1819, though we took the easier option of marbling rather than trying to copy the densely spotted pattern they had originally been (the painting was almost certainly not part of Adam's scheme but a later addition). The chairs were stripped of their later varnish and painted (as Chippendale suggests) to suit the colours of the room. *GH, 1994*

Epstein at work in his studio, 1939. ⟳

Epstein worked on Adam in between lucrative portrait commissions. It was a very personal project: "Into no other work had I merged myself so much, yet an Australian said to me: It is as if people had done this work and not just an individual".
Courtesy of Tate/the estate of Sir Jacob Epstein.

Epstein's 'Adam'

Jacob Epstein's great alabaster sculpture *Adam*, which dominates the room, has nothing to do with the 18th century at all. Made in the late 1930s, *Adam* was always controversial. Contemporary taste didn't know what to make of an image of the progenitor of us all (or so the Bible tells us) that was so physically explicit, so influenced by Epstein's fascination with African art and made by a Jew. *"Among us but not of us"*, a hostile critic said of Epstein. More than a hint of anti-semitism there I think.

Adam's travels took him half way round the world: from London to New York and South

Africa, until he ended up as part of Louis Tussaud's Collection of Anatomical Curiosities in a warehouse in Blackpool in the 1950s. From there he was acquired by my father for display as part of the great Epstein retrospective exhibition at the Edinburgh Festival in 1961, my father's first as Artistic Director. *Adam* arrived in Harewood shortly after and has stood in the Hall since 1976.

In 2010, *Adam* was a key work in an exhibition in the Royal Academy in London: *Modern British Sculpture.* He returned to Harewood cleaned, to be re-lit and displayed as he is now, literally the first thing you see as you walk through the front door.

DAVID LASCELLES (DL), 2012

"I feel ... that generations spoke through me, and the inner urge that took shape here was the universal one."
Jacob Epstein ⊙⊃

The Old Library

TO MOVE FROM THE POMP of Adam's Hall to the comfort of the Old Library is to exchange the formal for the domestic. Corinthian pilasters divide up the room, whose ceiling and walls have been repainted using what scraping the later over-painting revealed as Adam's original colour scheme – basically, green and white, with the frieze in contrasting grey. The ceiling is a typically elaborate, well-balanced Adam design, one of many to be seen throughout the House.

The eight Chippendale chairs were made for this room in the early 1770s. Above the bookcases and over the fireplace are paintings by Biagio Rebecca. The room also contains a fine late 18th century clock by Allen, with a dial revolving round the top; Chippendale's ingenious Library Steps (*illustrated below*) and a posthumous bust of Her Royal Highness Princess Mary (whose home Harewood was from 1929 until her death in 1965) by F.E. McWilliam (1909-1992). *GH, 1994*

Three decorative painters who worked with Adam at Harewood

Biagio Rebecca (1735-1808) was of Italian descent but lived and worked in England. He worked at Windsor Castle, Somerset House, Audley End and Kedleston, and specialised in the imitation of antique bas-relief, such as the example over the chimneypiece here. The pictures in the Gallery ceiling are also by him.

Angelica Kauffman (1741-1807) was born in Switzerland and became known as a youthful prodigy in Italy. Brought to England in 1765, she became in 1768 one of the founder members of the Royal Academy. Joshua Reynolds loved her but she was trapped into marriage by an impostor whom she had to pay off. In 1781 she married the Venetian **Antonio Zucchi** (1726-1795), who had travelled with Robert Adam through Italy, studying paintings and antiques and whom Adam invited to London where he became an A.R.A. in 1770. After enjoying a huge success with their mythological compositions and idyllic classical landscapes with ruins, the Zucchis retired to Italy in 1783. Harewood was one of several great houses they helped Robert Adam to adorn.

RICHARD BUCKLE (RB), 1980

Classical Scene
Biagio Rebecca,
*mounted into a pier glass
in the Gallery.* ⚲

Classical Scene
Angelica Kauffman,
*roundel in the ceiling of
the Music Room.* ⚲

The China Room

THIS PERFECTLY PROPORTIONED ROOM, called the Study by Adam in his original design, has also been a dressing room and a library. In 1958 we converted a cabinet for the display of porcelain, when the arched recesses were restored in accordance with Adam's drawings (now in the Soane Museum, London).

Joseph Rose carried out the ceiling and the plaster roundels, one of which, at the south end of the east wall, is particularly engaging in its fantasy, depicting a female centaur suckling her young. The relief over the chimneypiece is based on a famous ancient Roman painting from the first century AD known as the *Aldobrandini Marriage*: a bridegroom is shown waiting expectantly while his bride is made ready by female attendants. *GH, 1994*

Detail of Joseph Rose's bas-relief over the chimneypiece. ↪

Rose-pink Sèvres vase,
c. 1758. ⒼⒼ

Hand-painted floral
Coleport Fruit Stand,
c. 1845. Ⓖ

Harewood's China

HAREWOOD'S SÈVRES was collected in the early years of the 19th century by Edward Beau Lascelles. Although part of the collection was sold in 1965, there are many pieces of extreme beauty and rarity still at Harewood.

The Royal porcelain factory of Sèvres, founded in 1753, produced some of the most perfect pieces of china that have ever been modelled, fired, and adorned with gilt or painting, and the best of these were made before 1789, when the Revolution brought lower aesthetic standards. Indeed after the death in 1764 of Mme de Pompadour, whose inspired taste and steady patronage had animated the craftsmen of Sèvres, the imaginative richness of their porcelain began gradually to decrease.

For example, the rare and luscious rose-pink Sèvres was not made after Mme de Pompadour's death. Harewood can boast three pieces. Perhaps the most splendid is a shell-shaped vase painted by an unknown artist with a scene of two children with a fowling-net, imitated from an engraving by J.B. le Prince after Boucher. The two fan-shaped *vases hollandaises* with criss-cross pink and gold decoration may have been bought from the factory in 1758 by the Prince of Monaco. The apple-green pair with crossed ribbons are painted by Vieillard.

The splendid *bleu du roi* tea service (dated 1779) was a gift from the City of Paris to Queen Marie-Antoinette. The heavy gold foliage on the dark blue border of the tray sets off a painting of kingfisher delicacy, showing a group of peasants watching the antics of a monkey and three dogs in human clothing. All the scenes painted on this tea service by Pierre-André le Guay seem to evoke some remembered day when itinerant mountebanks came from over the hills and half the inhabitants of this hamlet ran to watch the performing animals, leaving the summer landscape littered with musical instruments, and their houses guarded by children or dogs. On the teapot a child buys a print of Louis XVI from a pedlar and on one of the four saucers a Punch sleeps under a tree beside a silent drum. *RB, 1980*

This room is sometimes used as part of the changing programme of exhibitions in the House, highlighting aspects of the collection or engaging in debate on contemporary cultural issues. The porcelain described here is therefore not always on display.

Tray from 'bleu du roi' tea service by Sèvres, 1779. Ⓖ

Princess Mary's Dressing Room

WHEN MY FATHER AND MOTHER came to live at Harewood in 1929 after my grandfather's death, Sir Herbert Baker (Lutyens' assistant on the grand project of New Delhi in India) was asked to design certain new features and supervise the restoration of others. This room was his largest new undertaking and, in the 'Adam revival' scheme he devised, he incorporated various decorative features taken from the demolished Harewood House in Hanover Square, London. The fireplace recess with its two cupboards containing some of my mother's collection of amber, rose quartz and jade, has in the apse a nymph inspired by Botticelli and designed by Sir Charles Wheeler. To the left and right of it are the Coats of Arms of Princess Mary and the 6th Earl of Harewood, the latter featuring Canning quarterings. The clock is by Sarton of Liège. *GH, 1994*

Expandable egg pendant
Carl Fabergé
George V & his children,
1912. ↻

Princess Mary & Henry,
6th Earl of Harewood
John Singer Sargent
(1856-1925). ↻

The sketch of Princess Mary was made only a few days before the artist died. She was suffering from hayfever at the time and always thought it made her look as if she had a cold.

Princess Mary on Portumna
Alfred Munnings
(1878-1959). ↻

Munnings was famously anti-modernist, but you can see the influence of the Impressionists in the way he has painted the light through the leaves in the background of this picture.

The East Bedroom

THIS WAS EDWIN LASCELLES' BEDROOM and the ceiling and frieze were designed by Robert Adam. But the main feature of the room, the Chinese wallpaper, was not part of the original scheme. It was hung by Chippendale's men in the Chintz Bedroom (on the 1st floor and not open to the public) in 1769. But later generations did not share the 18th century love for all things Chinese, so sometime in the first part of the 19th century, it was cut from the walls, rolled up in linen and put away in an outbuilding, where it lay for nearly 200 years. That it survived for so long is remarkable; that it survived in near perfect condition is astonishing.

Conservation work started in 2007 and was completed in 2008. Hand painted on fabric made from the pulp of the bark of the mulberry tree, this style of Chinese wallpaper was made exclusively for export to Europe. A continuous landscape runs round the room, showing a somewhat idealised version of traditional Chinese rural working life: making tea, growing rice, weaving silk, crafting porcelain. It is full of witty detail: a small dog barking at a visiting official; children playing in the street; a drunken villager the worse for wear after a hard day harvesting rice. The freshness and vibrancy of the colours can be ascribed, at least in part, to the fact that it was actually up on the walls at Harewood for a relatively short period of time, so not subject to the discolouring effects of age, sunlight, or wood and tobacco smoke. The conservators described it as *"one of the finest examples anywhere in the world"*.

The rest of the room was renovated at the same time as the wallpaper. New upholstery for the Chippendale bed and the curtains was made from hand-printed chintz fabric based on a mid 18th century Parisian design. The four green japanned pieces were also restored and reunited as a set – they are extremely rare examples of furniture in the Chinese style by Thomas Chippendale. *DL, 2012*

Famille Verte Chinese bowl with ormolu mount, early 18th century.

Detail of Chinese wallpaper.

Clothes press in the Chinese style by Thomas Chippendale, c. 1760.

The Collections Display Rooms

THE ROOMS ALONG the east wing of the House have always had a domestic use and in the 1930s they were converted into a modern bathroom and dressing room, part of the suite made for the 6th Earl and Princess Mary by Herbert Baker. They were then adapted in the 1990s to display Harewood's fine collection of watercolours, but the vulnerability of watercolours to sunlight means that we are not always able to display them. Like many great houses, Harewood has many objects not on permanent show so we often now use these rooms to highlight different aspects of Harewood's 'hidden' collections or to house temporary exhibitions. *DL, 2012*

Truth and Beauty
An exhibition of African tribal masks, shown as part of Harewood's commemoration of the Bicentenary of the Abolition of the Slave Trade in 2007. ⟳

Finding Adam
An exhibition about how Epstein's Adam came to Harewood. 2011. ⟳

Harewood's Watercolours

IN 1797, BEAU LASCELLES commissioned two young artists from London to paint watercolours of the House his father had recently inherited. One was JMW Turner (1775-1851), just 22 years old and starting to acquire a reputation as a promising architectural draughtsman. The other was Turner's friend and colleague Thomas Girtin (1775-1802). Beau is said to have preferred Girtin to Turner and it is interesting to compare their interpretations of the same view of Harewood House. With its gathering storm clouds and dramatic evening light, Girtin's version seems much more what we would now call 'Turneresque' than Turner's own rendition. Girtin died shortly afterwards and Turner was generous enough to say: *"If Tom Girtin had lived, I would have starved"*. Later, Beau also commissioned John Varley (1778-1842), watercolourist, astrologer and friend of William Blake, to paint the new House.

The Victorians regarded watercolours as an ephemeral medium, used by amateurs, and many of the paintings Beau commissioned were sold or given away to members of the

family. The 6th Earl and his wife Princess Mary (who was particularly fond of watercolours) were able to re-acquire some of these in the 1920s. He had already inherited watercolours from the Clanricarde collections in 1916, including scenes of Greece and Italy by Thomas Hartley Cromek (1809-1873) and volumes of delightful paintings by Charlotte Canning (1817-1861), aunt of the Marquess of Clanricarde, lady-in-waiting to the young Queen Victoria, and wife of the Viceroy of India. There is even one by Queen Victoria herself, dated 1848, copied from one of Lady Canning's own. *DL, 2012*

Harewood House from the Southeast
JMW Turner, *1798*. ⟳

Harewood House from the Southeast
Thomas Girtin, *1801*. ⟳

Lord Harewood's Sitting Room

Head of Marcella
Jacob Epstein, *1950.*

A gift from the artist's widow to my father, to thank him for his part in the retrospective of Epstein's work in Edinburgh in 1962. ☺

Arnold Schoenberg
Egon Schiele, *1917.*

My maternal grandfather, Erwin Stein, was a pupil of Schoenberg's in Vienna at the time this portrait was made. ⟳

IT WAS MY WIFE DIANE, an artist and curator by profession, who persuaded my father that his collection of 20th century art deserved its own showcase, to stand on its own merits alongside the other great historic works of art at Harewood. Lord Harewood's Sitting Room is that showcase.

My father described the room as *"A cheerful, unpretentious room, hung with pictures my wife and I have collected over the past thirty years, with no particular scheme in mind other than personal preference."*

He was being modest. My father and my stepmother bought paintings and sculptures by many important 20th century artists, such as Egon Schiele, Emil Nolde, Walter Sickert, Jacob Epstein and Henri Gaudier-Breszka. In addition, they acquired work by prominent artists who were also personal friends, like the Australians Sydney Nolan and Arthur Boyd, and the Indian MF Husain. *DL, 2012*

ARNOLD SCHÖNBERG

Chinese Landscape
Sydney Nolan, *1987.*

The great Australian artist Sydney Nolan was an old friend and compatriot of my stepmother. We showed a retrospective of his work in the Terrace Gallery in 1992, shortly before he died. ☺

Sunita and Anita
Jacob Epstein, *pencil drawing, c. 1930.* ⟳

Dravidian Heads
MF Husain, *1968.*

My father was supposed to open an exhibition of Husain's work in Mumbai in 1968, but was too ill to attend. The following morning, Husain arranged for the exhibition to be carried by his assistants to my father's hotel room and paraded past his sick bed one by one. This is the one he bought. ↻

The works on display change on a regular basis and are not necessarily those in the accompanying images. There are information sheets to tell you what is current, or please ask a House Steward who will gladly answer your questions.

The State Bedroom

A State Bedroom, reserved for visiting royalty or heads of state, was very much the fashion in a grand 18th century country house. This one was infrequently used – the future Queen Victoria in 1835 and Grand Duke Nicholas of Russia in 1816 are two of the rare instances – so it is perhaps unsurprising that Barry's 19th century alterations did away with it. The room became the sitting room of Barry's patron, Louisa 3rd Countess of Harewood, a function it retained for more than 100 years. I remember it as my grandmother Princess Mary's sitting room, her desk drawers full of old Christmas wrapping paper and recycled string.

Chippendale's magnificent bed was dismantled and put into storage, where it slumbered, half-forgotten, until it was rediscovered in the 1970s. It was not until 1999 that funding was found to restore it. This was a major undertaking. Although much of the ornately carved and painted decoration had been carefully stored, nearly 150 years had passed and quite a lot was missing. Nobody knew exactly what the bed would have looked like in the first place –

Chippendale never made another one like it and there were of course no photographs. The end result is a tribute to the skill and imagination of the furniture historians and the expert craftsmen and women who worked on it. It now stands as one of Chippendale's most extraordinary creations, a masterpiece of English furniture.

Two more of Chippendale's finest pieces, designed for the State Dressing Room (now the Spanish Library), are also here: a marquetry satinwood secretaire and *The Diana and Minerva* commode (*below*), which, with its intricate ivory inlay, elegant lines and drawers that whisper shut like an airlock, is often referred to as his single greatest work.

Restoring the State Bedroom to its former glory involved more than just the bed: the ceiling colours are once again those chosen by Robert Adam, the green silk on the walls and on the bed is a copy of the original. We also restored the original door configuration so you can now enjoy, once again, the spectacular *enfilade* and see through every room along the south side of the House. *DL, 2012*

The Spanish Library

THIS ROOM HAS BEEN many things in the life of Harewood House. Originally the State Dressing Room, ensuite with the State Bedroom next door, Barry transformed it into a Victorian library. After that, the room was used as a Breakfast Room for many years and was even briefly my father's study, with the room used for family gatherings (the Library) on one side and my grandmother's Sitting Room (now the State Bedroom) on the other.

Between the tall bookcases and the ceiling is a 17th century wall-covering of Spanish leather put there by the 6th Earl, hence the room's name (though the leather is actually from the Netherlands). There are busts from various periods on top of the bookcases and above you is another fine Adam ceiling. It is also worth noting the two 'secret' doors disguised as bookshelves: the one between this room and the State Bedroom and one in the far corner to the left of the fireplace.

There are more than 11,000 books in the three libraries at Harewood. The oldest are three volumes published in Florence in 1568, Vasari's seminal works about the Renaissance: *Le Vite de' più eccelente pittori, scultori e architettori (Lives of the Most Excellent Painters, Sculptors and Architects)*, and the most recent are from the late 20th century. Their cataloguing and conservation is a massive and ongoing project. *DL, 2012*

Lives of the Painters
Georgio Vasari
published in 1568. G

The view from the Library back to the Hall, Epstein's Adam centre stage. ⬆

The Library

THE LIBRARY, known in the past as the Saloon, is now a mainly Victorian room dominated by Barry's imposing mahogany bookcases with their brass inlay and marble chair rail. It maintains stylistic contact with an earlier century through Adam's spectacular ceiling together with his chimneypieces and plaster overmantels with their round, sculptured reliefs by William Collins. *"Some Adam ceilings are rectilinear and heroic, such as that in the Hall, others are delicate, such as that in the East Bedroom; this one might be described as 'symphonic', with its motifs and colours which ebb, flow, swell, repeat themselves and dissemble into one tremendous scheme"*, says Richard Buckle with some justification in an earlier guide book.

which since Barry's transformation has been the central living room of the House and is still used for family gatherings today.

There are four objects supplied by the Royal Clockmaker, Benjamin Vulliamy. The ormolu-mounted marble-cased clock (on the chimneypiece) is signed and was made about 1796; the bronze tazza on the table in the right-hand alcove was supplied in 1804; and the black, marble and ormolu-mounted lamps are also signed and dated 'AD 1811'.

The four decorative landscapes high on the east and west walls are by Nicholas Dall (a Dane, who died in London in 1777). They are of four local views: Harewood Castle, Aysgarth Force, Knaresborough and Richmond. Another picture of Harewood Castle by Michael 'Angelo' Rooker (1746-1801) hangs over the north door.

In the last years of the 18th century and long before Barry's alteration, Harewood's new owner must already have had ideas of turning the room from a central concourse into something more habitable. Two doors were suppressed and replaced by pictures of Plompton Rocks by JMW Turner, his earliest oil paintings (1798) and the only oils by him in the House. *GH, 1994*

Plaster decoration above fireplace by William Collins. ⌒

Plompton Rocks
JMW Turner, 1798.

This is still a place where people walk and go boating as they did in Turner's time. Beau Lascelles paid him £32 for this and its companion piece, also in the Library. ↻

When I first knew the room, the ceiling was green with elements of blue, red and gold, and the walls were covered in dark blue and chocolate paint with a regular gold pattern. Bookcases and paint together produced a note of unintended gloom, and there was little reconciliation between walls and ceiling. The choice of terracotta as a colour basis was made in 1958 in an attempt to accommodate Barry's monumentality and Adam's fantasy in a room

Adelina Patti
Franz Winterhalter
1805-1873. ☉

The Yellow Drawing Room

CONSISTENCY OF MOTIF was something Adam regularly sought. In this room the star and circle of the carpet echo without slavishly copying the ceiling and design motifs repeat throughout.

In the 19th and early 20th centuries, the room was used as a Billiard Room, but it was originally known as the Yellow Drawing Room. Edwin Lascelles, after work on decorating the House had begun, bought yellow silk for the walls and Adam was obliged to revamp his colour scheme for the ceiling. A day book for

September 1769 mentions painting *"a specimen of colours for Mr Adam's approbation".*

Two splendid looking glasses by Thomas Chippendale dominate, with a third, over the fireplace, by Chippendale's son (also called Thomas) who completed the Harewood commission after his father's death in 1779. The paintings are exclusively of women, including a delightful portrait of the great 19th century opera singer, *Adelina Patti* by Franz Winterhalter.

Let's end with the furniture. There is an exceptionally fine Chippendale commode, *The Three Graces*, the third piece of the set that would have been in the State Dressing Room (the other two are now in the State Bedroom). The other piece of particular interest is a modern one, a games table made for my wife and me by David Linley in 2004, the first furniture commission at Harewood since Chippendale's time. Inside is a hand-painted chessboard by Charlotte, Lady Canning, depicting scenes from India. *GH, 1994 / DL, 2012*

The Three Graces
commode
Thomas Chippendale
c. 1773.

Above the commode is one of the Chippendale mirrors restored in the 1990s. More ornate decoration is reflected in its glass. ☉

The Cinnamon Drawing Room

JOHN JEWELL'S EARLY GUIDEBOOK tells us that this room was originally hung with white damask and bordered with gold. It was known as the White Drawing Room and featured no fewer than five looking glasses as well as two full-length family portraits. The white silk was later replaced by green, which gradually faded until the decision to concentrate family portraits in this room prompted the present cinnamon background.

The ram's head pier glasses now here were originally in the Dining Room (before it was redesigned and enlarged by Barry to a scale which would no longer accommodate them). In 1989 they were reunited with the console tables which properly belong underneath them so that they now stand together for the first time for nearly 150 years. These were the first of several pairs of mirrors to have Chippendale's elaborate ornamentation – removed by the Victorians – restored before being reintroduced in places of honour in the House.

The paintings in the cove and centre of Adam's ceiling are not part of his original design, but were added in 1852 by Alfred Stevens. *GH, 1994*

Lady Harrington
Joshua Reynolds
(1723-1792)
Edwin's stepdaughter as Aurora goddess of the dawn.

The paintings in the main picture are, left to right:

Henrietta, Lady Harewood
Thomas Hoppner
(1758-1810).

Henry, 2nd Earl of Harewood
Joshua Reynolds *(above).*

Edward Lascelles
Unknown artist
Said to be of Edward, brother of Henry the West Indian merchant (below).

Anne, Countess of Harewood with her Infant Daughter
Joshua Reynolds *(above).*

Lady Louisa Lascelles
Thomas Lawrence
(1769-1830)
Preliminary sketch for a portrait. (below).

Detail of ram's head pier table by Thomas Chippendale.

Paintings

Most English country houses have interesting family portraits and these are representative of the finest portrait painters of their time. We move them around from time to time so please refer to the room sheet or ask a House Steward to locate what is where. These illustrations are of just some of them. *DL, 2012*

Edwin Lascelles
Joshua Reynolds
(1723-1792).

Edwin, with his new house in the landscape behind him. ⌒

Lady Worsley, *Lady Harrington's sister (see previous page), one of Reynolds' finest portraits.* ⌒

Seymour Fleming was a wealthy young heiress of 17 when she married Sir Richard Worsley. After some years of marriage, she eloped with Captain George Bisset, a young officer from the South Hampshire militia (commanded by her husband and whose uniform she is wearing in Reynolds' portrait). Worsley was furious and took her and her lover to court under the 18th century law of 'criminal conversation'. This is based on the concept, extraordinary to us now, that a wife was her husband's property and if another man took her away from him, this was theft, the theft of something with a quantifiable value. The 'thief', in this case Captain Bisset, would have to pay compensation, a sum to be decided by the courts.

Worsley demanded £20,000, an unprecedentedly high sum, and one which would have totally ruined the couple. Seymour no longer had access to her own fortune, which all belonged to her husband for as long as they were married.

Rather than face financial ruin Seymour took the extraordinary step of ruining her own reputation. She claimed her husband had encouraged the affair, as he had others before it, more or less acting as her pimp. He liked, it seemed, to watch. The case hinged round a bizarre incident at a bathhouse in Maidstone, where Sir Richard was witnessed helping Bisset watch Seymour inside, naked as she took the waters. The case was a huge scandal. Worsley won, but instead of £20,000, he was awarded just one shilling.

Edward, 1st Earl of Harewood *in Van Dyck fancy dress aged 22, also by Reynolds.* ↻

George Canning as a Boy
Thomas Gainsborough
(1727-1788).

Probably painted as Canning left Eton, one of Gainsborough's last works. ↻

Edward, Viscount Lascelles
John Hoppner
(1758-1810).

This is Beau Lascelles, the patron of Turner and Girtin and collector of much of the china in the House. ↻

Hubert, Marquess of Clanricarde
Henry Tonks (1862-1937).

Hubert Clanricarde left his considerable fortune to his great-nephew Harry, who became the 6th Earl and acquired the paintings in the Gallery with his unexpected inheritance. ↻

The Gallery

"THIS ROOM EXTENDS over the whole west end of the House, and is 76 feet 10 inches by 24 feet 3 inches, 21 feet 3 inches high; it is truly elegant, and presents such a show of magnificence and art as eye hath seldom seen and words cannot describe" – so some 50 years after it was built wrote John Jewell in the earliest guide book to Harewood.

It was one of Adam's most magnificent achievements, but not immune on that account to alterations under Barry's aegis. Columns supporting the central arches of the three triple windows were replaced by brackets (a favourite device of Barry's, it would appear); and the chimneypiece, for which Adam's design is dated 1776, was removed to the Dining Room and two Victorian replacements installed. We restored the chimneypiece to its original position in 1990, and the main windows are again graced by the pillars and pilasters which, says Jewell's guide book, were "painted by Mr Hutchinson, of London, in imitation of the verd antique marble and admirably transcribed from a table in the same room".

Adam drew the design for the ceiling in 1769 and Rose executed it within a couple of years. The exploits – amorous, war-like or simply ceremonial – of Greek gods and goddesses are depicted on it and on the four decorative oval paintings above the mirrors between the windows. There is some debate about whether these are by Angelica Kauffman or Biagio Rebecca or whether they collaborated on them together, as they quite often did.

All the mirrors and the elegant torchères stand to the credit of Thomas Chippendale; the marble-topped console tables with their rams' heads and lions' feet on which the mirrors rest are by his son, Thomas Chippendale the Younger. Crowning Chippendale's achievement here – a celebrated feature of the room – are the pelmets, made of wood and beautifully carved to imitate a heavy material – the only 'curtains' the room was intended to have. GH 1994

Carved wooden curtain pelmets by Thomas Chippendale. No others are thought to exist. ◔

Cupid
Marble statue by John Gibson (1790-1866). ◔

Porcelain

The Gallery houses the famous Harewood collection of Chinese Porcelain. It is instructive to consider the history of these fragile works of art.

By the time of the Ming Emperors the various refinements of turning, carving, engraving, painting in underglaze, crackling, firing, enamelling and gilding had been perfected at the factory of Ching-Tê-Chên, near Peking. These vases and bowls, either in plain colours – celadon green, *clair de lune* (pale moonlight blue), *sang de boeuf* (bull's blood) or lavender – or enamelled with cocks, peacocks, peonies or plum blossom in the styles known as *famille verte* and *famille rose*, were mostly executed during the reigns of the emperors K'ang Hsi, Yung Cheng and Ch'ien Lung, between 1662 and 1795. Exported to France, they were used almost as a base on which French craftsmen in ormolu (gilded bronze) could demonstrate their invention and skill; they were given richly chased rims, pedestals and handles in styles ranging from the florid rococo of the mid 18th century to the severe and rigid neo-classicism of the Empire. As their aristocratic collectors fell victim to the Revolution, so these treasures appeared in the Paris salerooms; and in 1802, when many English collectors took advantage of the Peace of Amiens to dash over to Paris, the collection was begun by Beau Lascelles who brought it to his London home in Hanover Square, and eventually to Yorkshire. In addition to those decorated in France, three blue Chinese vases were mounted with ormolu ornaments for Beau in 1806 by Vulliamy.

RB, 1980

Paintings

WHEN THE HOUSE was first built, there seem to have been few if any pictures in this room. Edwin Lascelles must have relied on the decorative skills of Adam and Chippendale to make an effect, but by the 1820s it had become the focus for family portraits. In 1989-1990, it was decided not only to redecorate the room, which had become shabby with age and as a result of floods from the floor above it (to say nothing of a fire at the end of the 19th century), but to concentrate in the Gallery the Renaissance pictures collected in the decade after the 1st World War by the 6th Earl. Some have been sold to pay death duties but what remain are to be found here.

A comprehensive description of all the paintings in this room can be found on the room sheets. These are just some of them.

The paintings in the main picture are, top to bottom & left to right:

St Catherine of Alexandria
Attributed to Filippino Lippi *(c. 1457–1504).*

An Admiral
Tintoretto (Jacopo Robusti) *(1518-1594)*

The figure is by Tintoretto himself, the background (of the port of Alexandria) probably by his assistants. The subject was long thought to be a famous Venetian admiral; now experts are not so sure.

Madonna and Child
Lazzaro Bastiani *(c. 1430–1512).*

Portrait of a Gentleman
Veronese (Paolo Caliari) *(c. 1528-1588).*

Painted in Veronese's last years and thought to be of a member of the prominent Venetian Soranzo family.

Allegory
El Greco (Doménicos Theotocópoulos). *(c. 1541-1614).*

See page 58 for detailed information.

St Anthony of Padua
Neapolitan School *(date unknown).*

Francis I
Titian (Tiziano Vecellio), *(1485-1576).*

This painting was known to have been in Titian's studio when he died and is probably a ricordo (a copy for future reference) that the artist made from the portrait now in the Louvre. The profile of the French King is very distinctive.

Madonna and Child with Donor
Giovanni Bellini, *(1430/40-1516).*

This was a favourite subject of Bellini's.

Madonna and Child with the infant St John
Mariotto Albertinelli *(Florentine, 1474-1515).*

Albertinelli specialised in small devotional pictures, which were much sought after by his wealthy Florentine patrons. ☍

Allegory
El Greco (Doménicos Theotocópoulos), (c. 1541–1614).

There are three versions of this intriguing, enigmatic, mysterious work. The earliest (probably painted in Rome c. 1570–1575) is now in the Prado in Madrid; this version was painted soon after El Greco's arrival in Toledo 1577–1578; and a later example (also painted in Toledo c. 1585) is now in Edinburgh. ⟳

St Jerome in the Desert
Cima (Giovanni Battista Cima da Conegliano) (c. 1460–1518).

St Jerome prays in a parched but golden landscape, guarded by his lion and surrounded by birds and other animals, in a state of divine natural harmony. ↪

Madonna and Child with St John the Baptist and St Jerome
Vincenzo Catena,
(Venetian, 1480-1556).

Once in the collection of William Beckford, West Indian trader and builder of the ill-fated Fonthill Abbey, when it was thought to be by Bellini, Catena's teacher. G

Christ at the Column
Unknown artist
(*probably Tuscan, late 15th century*).

This picture once belonged to the poet Robert Browning, who mentions it in his poem 'Old Pictures in Florence':

*Could not the ghost with the close red cap,
My Pollaiuolo, the twice a craftsman,
Save me a sample, give me the hap
Of a muscular Christ that shows the draughtsman?*

Contemporary scholars are now fairly certain that this fine painting is not in fact by Pollaiuolo at all but by another, unknown artist. G

The Rape of the Sabine Women
Appollonio di Giovanni
(*worked in Florence between 1445 and 1465*).

This, together with 'The Generosity of Scipio' (not shown), were originally fronts of cassoni or marriage chests. ⟳

The Dining Room

BARRY'S CHANGES TO THIS ROOM in the 1840s are the most radical anywhere on the State Floor. He raised the ceiling and changed the shape of the room – Robert Adam's original plans are in the Sir John Soane Museum in London. Nothing of this scheme remains in situ, with the rather significant exception of the Chippendale furniture: a fine set of dining room chairs and two superb side-tables, urn-topped pedestals and a wine cooler. These are among Chippendale's finest pieces and very much made to be used: the wine coolers and urns are lined with lead and one of the pedestals conceals racks to keep plates warm.

The present chimneypiece, with the head of Bacchus the god of food and wine in its centre, is the third one this room has had. The one Adam designed for it disappeared without trace in Barry's alterations and was replaced by the one that was originally in the Gallery and then returned there in 1990.

The room is full of portraits of the Earls and Countesses of Harewood, with one exception, the portrait of the statesman and Prime Minister George Canning by Thomas Lawrence (1769-1830). Canning was the grandfather of Elizabeth de Burgh, wife of the 4th Earl. *DL, 2012*

Princess Mary
Oswald Birley
(1880-1952).

This portrait of my grandmother was painted in 1922 as a wedding present from the tenants on the Harewood Estate. ↷

Wine cooler and side-table by Thomas Chippendale, c.1770. ↻

Urn-topped pedestal by Thomas Chippendale, c. 1770. ↻

Henry, 6ᵗʰ Earl of Harewood
John St Helier Lander, 1916.

Harry was painted while on convalescent leave from the 1ˢᵗ World War, wearing his Grenadier Guard greatcoat. He holds his wounded right arm rather awkwardly hidden behind him. I like to think this was painted just before his fateful meeting with his great-uncle Hubert. The dates certainly fit. ➲

Henry, 3ʳᵈ Earl of Harewood
Francis Grant
(1803-1878).

Henry died as a result of a hunting accident, like his father. He was wounded at the battle of Waterloo (his Waterloo medal hangs below the painting) on June 18ᵗʰ 1815. My grandfather Harry, the 6ᵗʰ Earl, was wounded in battle during the 1ˢᵗ World War on June 18ᵗʰ 1915. My father, the 7ᵗʰ Earl, was wounded in battle during the 2ⁿᵈ World War on June 18ᵗʰ 1944. ↷

Mrs Hale
Joshua Reynolds, 1764. ⊙

Zucchi's painting on the wall; Sevres porcelain and Sotiau's clock on the table; Chippendale's sofa and chairs upholstered in Beauvais tapestry. ↻

The Music Room

THE MUSIC ROOM is the room in the House least changed from Robert Adam's original concept. It is a classic example of the coordinated 'overall decorative scheme' that Adam always strived for, with fine work by some of his most important and most frequent collaborators.

Firstly, Thomas Chippendale whose sofas and chairs here were originally in the State Bedroom and State Dressing Room. All are covered in Beauvais tapestry. Chippendale is also responsible for the frame of the large painting by Joshua Reynolds above the fireplace. This is a family portrait: of Mrs Hale, sister-in-law of the 1st Earl. She and her children are depicted as characters from Milton's poem *L'allegro*. Another of Adam's favourite collaborators, Angelica Kauffman, painted the ceiling roundels of a range of classical scenes and her husband Antonio Zucchi made the four large wall-mounted paintings which Richard Buckle describes as being *"like windows opening onto views of a half-imaginary Mediterranean"*. The lilac tinge in the sunset clouds is picked up in one of the colours Adam used in the wall and ceiling borders.

The carpet is one of only two original Adam designs in the House (the other is in the Yellow Drawing Room) and echoes the pattern of the ceiling.

There are a couple of later additions - the two console tables on either side of the room are Regency, the Sèvres porcelain is part of Beau Lascelles' collection, and the ormolu-mounted striking clock by Nicolas Sotiau is late Louis XVI – but overall the room is still pretty much as Adam intended it. *GH, 1980*

If anyone asks 'Where's the music?' he must be answered in the words of Keats: 'Heard melodies are sweet, but those unheard are sweeter.' There are lyres woven in the pattern of the carpet, more lyres, pipes and trumpets carved on the marble chimney; and there are ormolu trophies of musical instruments on the magnificent Sèvres clock, which may have belonged to Marie-Antoinette. The central ceiling painting depicts Midas presiding over a musical contest between lyre-playing Apollo and Marsyas, who favoured woodwind. In the Zucchi painting to the right of the fireplace a band is performing at the top of the stairs; and in his painting on the west wall, there are brigands playing pipes, while a tearful peasant in a red cloak fingers a lute, accompanied with tragic abandon by a lady on the triangle. In the Reynolds portrait group, three of Euphrosyne's children are letting rip on pipe and timpani, while a fourth, deafened by all these painted orchestras, is saying 'Sssh!'
RB, 1980

Below Stairs

IT TOOK A SMALL ARMY of people to look after a house the size of Harewood. This is where that army worked: the sculleries, kitchens, servants' halls and parlours that were the engine room of the English country house, the legs paddling furiously under the water to keep the swan gliding serenely on the surface.

John Carr was a very practical architect and he took great pains to ensure that the working areas at Harewood were efficient and well designed. Later, Charles Barry's Victorian alterations introduced many modernisations such as a new kitchen range and a state-of-the-art bell system, as well as creating new sculleries and servants' bedrooms. As a result Below Stairs is unusually light and well aired for its time, with easy access between the working areas and, crucially, a very short distance from the kitchens to the State Dining Room upstairs. As many as forty would have worked here in Victorian times and in the 1930s there was still a staff of twenty seven: footmen, cooks and maids, all presided over by a head butler and housekeeper.

Below Stairs, opened by Princess Anne, The Princess Royal, in 2004, takes you through all the key rooms. This highlights some of the main features. *DL, 2012*

The Kitchen. ⌂

The Pastry Room. ⌂

The Kitchen

The Head Cook (always men and mostly French in the Victorian era, mainly women after that) was one of the best-paid members of staff at Harewood and would have had a team of at least three kitchen maids working for them, plus a full-time baker. The Cook's room was above the kitchen and had a window high on the wall to keep an eye on what was happening below.

The wooden table in the middle of the room dates from when the House was built, the charcoal stove under the window is Victorian, and the large range (*right*), made by Benham and Sons of London, dates from the 1930s and was used to capacity during the 2nd World War, when Harewood was a convalescent hospital. It was apparently very hot and awkward to work with.

65

The Servants' Hall

This is where the servants ate, with men and women sitting along wooden benches at separate tables, the Housekeeper at the head of one and the Butler at the other.

The most striking feature of the room is high on the walls: the bell boards (*right*). What you see today was installed as part of the Victorian modernisations and was still in use until the 1940s. Bells were a necessity in a house as large as Harewood, the most efficient way to communicate between upstairs and downstairs in the days before telephones. Before that, servants would have had to wait outside the door to be summoned, or even in the room itself, so they represented a major labour-saving device – servants could continue with duties below stairs rather than lingering indefinitely upstairs – as well as a greater degree of privacy for the family and guests.

PICTURE GALLERY. DRAWING ROOM. BILLIARD ROOM. WEST No 4 No 5 BATH ROOM. WEST WING. WEST WI

George 'Bertie' Robinson *was born in St Vincent in the West Indies in 1880. In the 1901 census he is recorded as one of three footmen serving in the house.* ↺

The Still Room
This area was used to prepare preserves and cordials as well as for laying up trays for breakfast or tea. ↺↺

Princess Mary with her sons George and Gerald, *1926.* ↺

Princess Mary pruning the roses, *c. 1960.* ↺

Princess Mary's Garden Room

Princess Mary lived at Harewood for more than 30 years. She moved here with her husband the 6th Earl in 1929 and died here while walking round the lake with her son in 1965. She was the daughter of one King (George V), sister to two more (Edward VIII and George VI) and aunt to our present Queen Elizabeth II.

She performed her Royal and official duties with great diligence but her real love was for Harewood and for the classic country pursuits of riding, gardening and the Estate. These rooms feature a changing display of items celebrating her life, including things she collected or was given, artefacts reflecting her country interests, and private letters and papers.

The Terrace Gallery

Clockwise from top right:

Deep Waters
Susan Derges, 2004

New Work
Jason Brooks, 2001

Magnesium Bird
Sutapa Biswas, 2004

Retrospective
Sidney Nolan, 1992

Two States
Antony Gormley, 2011

THE PROJECT TO CREATE the Terrace Gallery began in 1988. The Sub-Hall, opening on to the Terrace on the south front of the House, was panelled and lit to become a contemporary gallery space for temporary exhibitions. It opened to the public in 1989 and since that time has shown a changing programme of exhibitions by a wide range of artists at different stages of their careers.

The Terrace Gallery was the first gallery space dedicated to contemporary art to open in an English country house. It is part of a continuum of support and patronage of contemporary art at Harewood. Turner and Girtin were in their early twenties, at the beginning of their careers, when they were commissioned by Beau Lascelles in 1797. More recently Epstein's *Adam*, brought here by my father-in-law in the 1970s, is now the first thing visitors see on entering the House.

From the opening of the Terrace Gallery a more extensive programme has developed across the wider landscape of Harewood. *Harewood Contemporary* locates new works alongside the historic collections in various rooms in the House, in the Church, in the Gardens and the landscape as well as in the Terrace Gallery.

DIANE HOWSE, COUNTESS OF HAREWOOD, 2012

Landscape

HAREWOOD HOUSE is very much a building in a landscape and the transition between Capability Brown's carefully cultivated 'natural' setting and the House itself is the Gardens. There are separate booklets (either already existing or imminent) on different aspects of Harewood's Gardens, so this is just a verbal and pictorial introduction.

at dusk, when the owl flies and thought keeps company with feeling

Harewood Contemporary

Many projects have happened in the
landscape over the years. Some were
temporary installations but three still visible
today are: Poem in the Owl Seat, outside the
Walled Garden *(far left)* by Thomas A Clark;
Eve, a golden tree to be viewed through
golden opera glasses from the Yellow Drawing
Room *(centre)* by Kate Davis; *What use is a
sign if we know the Way?* in the West Garden
(top) by Leo Fitzmaurice.

The Terrace

The most spectacular manifestation of Charles Barry's changes to Harewood in the 1840s, the Terrace's Italianate style and intricate geometric flowerbeds are typical of the Victorian taste for formal gardens. By the late 1950s the expense of maintaining it had become unaffordable and the box hedging was removed, the parterre grassed over and the fountains filled with soil and planted. It was not till 1994 that Barry's original design was fully restored, with the help of grants from English Heritage and the European Commission. The original central fountain collapsed in the hard winter of 1983 and Astrid Zydower's *Orpheus* replaced it.

The Bird Garden

Spreading down the steep slope that runs down from Carr's Stable block to the Lake, the Harewood Bird Garden was created in 1970 by my father and stepmother as an additional attraction for family visitors. Home to a wide range of rare or endangered species from around the world, the Bird Garden is involved with several captive breeding programmes as well as delighting the child in all of us with its penguins, flamingos, owls and waterfowl.

The Himalayan Garden

Formerly known as the Rock Garden, this area was a favourite of my grandfather and grandmother. The collections of rhododendrons and primulas they created form the basis of the Himalayan Garden. In 2004 I invited a group of monks from the Himalayan Kingdom of Bhutan to build a Stupa – a Buddhist monument – there. A newly created path leads you down a gorge, across the garden with views of its wide variety of Himalayan flora and over a Chinese-style bridge, before inviting you to walk round the Stupa (three times in a clockwise direction is traditional).

The Walled Garden

The oldest garden still being cultivated at Harewood, building began in 1755, earlier even than Harewood House itself. Pineapples, bananas, nectarines and other exotic tropical produce were cultivated in its hothouses, with vegetables and indigenous fruits growing outside. About 1/3 of its seven acres was re-opened to the public in 1999 after the redevelopment of the vegetable borders either side of the central path and the creation of *Spiral Meadow* by Diane Howse. Now vegetables for the café and shops grow there, with hops along the top wall, fruit trees in the western section and a display beehive by the west wall.

I HOPE YOU HAVE ENJOYED your visit or this book (or both).
If you care about Harewood and want to help look after its future,
why not become a Harewood Member (details below). All proceeds
go to the Harewood House Trust, the educational charitable trust
that looks after Harewood for the public benefit.
Please visit again – as often as you like.
DAVID LASCELLES, Earl of Harewood

FEEL AT HOME AT HAREWOOD
WITH HAREWOOD MEMBERSHIP

For more details:
www.harewood.org/membership
0113 218 1000

Give Harewood as a gift
like Harewood, love Harewood membership